essential careers™

A CAREER AS AN
EVENT COORDINATOR

BARBARA KRASNER

ROSEN
PUBLISHING®

NEW YORK

Published in 2015 by The Rosen Publishing Group, Inc.
29 East 21st Street, New York, NY 10010

Library of Congress Cataloging-in-Publication Data

Krasner, Barbara.
A career as an event coordinator/Barbara Krasner.
    pages cm.—(Essential careers)
Includes bibliographical references and index.
ISBN 978-1-4777-7878-4 (library bound)
1. Special events—Planning—Vocational guidance—Juvenile literature. I. Title.
GT3405.K73 2015
394.2023—dc23

                       2014008551

contents

INTRO

Becoming an event coordinator can be rewarding for those who are willing to work hard, plan, and keep track of details, and who take joy in making clients and guests happy.

DUCTION

S andy Sloane of Rochester, New York, has been coordinating events most of her life. She started as a child, planning birthday parties for herself and her sister. It helped that their birthdays were close to holidays—Valentine's Day and Halloween. Her mother always added a theme to the party. That made it easier to decide on food, decorations, and goodie bags. Sloane said, "I learned very early about how to incorporate a theme into an event to make it fun...When my friends at school couldn't stop talking about how fun my parties were and how they always looked forward to them, I knew I had found my life's passion."

The job of an event coordinator, also known as an event planner, is to create memorable events. Corporations, universities, hospitals, and many more organizations rely on event coordinators. It doesn't matter whether you live in a large city or a small town. Event coordination is needed everywhere. According to the U.S. Bureau of Labor Statistics, careers in event planning are expected to grow at a rate faster than most jobs in America.

Many roads can lead to a career in event coordination. Many already have experience without knowing it. For example, anyone who has worked as a waiter in a restaurant already knows how to listen to and satisfy a customer. Someone who has volunteered to help raise funds for a school knows the importance of working with others toward a common goal. People who have helped out at an art museum already know how art can lift a person's mood or spirit. Some people have an eye for color. That helps them choose a decorating style. A good writer will be able to easily inform clients about events as well as be able to describe an event in detail so the event coordinator's vision for the event can be shared.

A career in event coordination allows people to use a wide range of skills and talents. To be successful takes determination, creativity, and the ability to handle many things at once. One person may not know everything, but if he or she knows who to call for help, that's part of the teaming necessary for success.

This resource outlines the different types of events, the skills one needs to become an event coordinator, what an event coordinator does, and how best to prepare for and break into an event coordinator career. Get ready to learn about available training and education programs. Finally, the resource discusses what lies ahead for the industry. Throughout, you'll read about real-life event planners and get a real feel for the day-to-day activities.

Each project an event coordinator takes on has its own unique personality. There are sacrifices. Long hours, attention to the smallest detail, and demanding clients as well as guests can be stressful. But there are rewards, too. Seeing satisfied clients smile and knowing you've made a difference can be well worth the work.

Opportunity awaits!

chapter 1

WHAT IS EVENT COORDINATION?

Wherever people get together for a meeting or event, someone needs to be in charge of organizing everything. That someone is the event coordinator, also called an event planner, special event coordinator, private event coordinator, or a meeting planner. The event coordinator is someone who plans, runs, and manages meetings and events for a living. The event coordinator takes a theme or a concept and makes it come alive at an event, influencing the lives of many people. The event coordinator is someone on whom many people depend to create and deliver an impressive event.

The event coordinator can work in a variety of industries and places, including restaurants, banquet halls, hotels, party-planning companies, large corporations, hospitals, universities, museums, and small businesses. In a hotel, for instance, an event coordinator books ballrooms and other special-function rooms. In a hospital, college, or corporation, an event coordinator plans functions for training, professional meetings, and celebrations.

An event coordinator doesn't just plan the event. He or she attends it, too, to make sure the event runs smoothly. The event coordinator also handles any problems as they arise. And problems certainly do arise.

Event coordinators handle every client's needs, including planning outdoor or indoor events and informal or formal parties.

Event planning is a relatively new field. In the past, mothers and daughters, harried employees, and business owners had to figure out for themselves how to organize an event. They had no training and no idea where to start. Times have changed. Professional organizations and magazines help the event coordinator learn new practices and stay on top of trends. There are degree and certification programs.

As an event coordinator, you will face new challenges every day. You will grow and learn. You will push your creativity beyond where you thought you could. And while this is happening, you will provide satisfaction to your clients. Event coordination is one of the most exciting and rewarding careers today.

Top 10 Cities for Event Planners

According to the U.S. Bureau of Labor Statistics outlook for 2012 to 2022, the number of event planning jobs is expected to increase 32 percent from the bureau's 2010–2020 outlook. It estimates a 33 percent growth rate over a ten-year period, much faster than other industries. The bureau also identified the following cities as offering tremendous opportunities for event coordinators:

New York, NY – 5,680 jobs
Washington, DC – 5,100 jobs
Chicago, IL – 2,300 jobs
Los Angeles, CA – 1,840 jobs
Atlanta, GA – 1,690 jobs
Boston, MA – 1,270 jobs
Dallas, TX – 1,480 jobs
Philadelphia, PA – 1,270 jobs
Minneapolis, MN – 1,240 jobs
Phoenix, AZ – 1,200 jobs

EVENTS IN A TENT? WHY NOT?

Today, an event coordinator can choose from a vast array of venues. Traditional locations, like hotel ballrooms and convention centers, are still top choices. Other venues include restaurants, museums, parks, historic sites, beaches, gardens, country clubs, golf courses, schools, shopping malls, art galleries, sports arenas, zoos, stage theaters, movie theaters, and ranches.

Many cities have their own convention centers and stadiums that can be used for all kinds of special events. For example, the Jacob Javits Center in New York City was the chosen location for nine events in January 2014 alone. These included a boat show; several fashion shows; a convention of the National Retail Federation; an exposition ("expo") for the heating, ventilation, and air conditioning industry; a textile show; and a home and lifestyle gift show. The possibilities are seemingly endless.

Coordinating destination events, like a beachfront wedding, requires careful attention to detail and backup plans if the weather doesn't cooperate.

EVENTS IN ALL SHAPES AND SIZES

There are all types of events that need planning and management. They come in all shapes and sizes. For example, seminars and workshops usually invite attendees to actively participate. Smaller than a conference, their goal is to stimulate conversation and to educate. These events can last just a single day or be multiple-day events.

Many corporations have their own event planners on staff. American Express, for example, has more than one thousand employees doing this kind of work. Corporations can also hire an outside firm to manage their events. Corporate events can take place at their own location or at a hotel or even a theme park in another state where they might be hosting a sales meeting. They could take a year to plan or they could have very tight deadlines.

WHEN REALITY MEETS FANTASY

Donte Clavo had his own idea about a career in event planning. Meeting famous people. Selecting fabulous food. He'd gotten hooked on the idea as a student at Howard University, where he helped plan a longstanding event. There was music, dancing, and food. Students, graduates, and the community were invited.

After graduation, he accepted a job planning events for a not-for-profit business. It was hard work coordinating an event. He had to deal with a lot of people and a lot of different personalities, all to create a single great event. He dug in his heels and stuck it out. He told Lisa Plummer Savas on the Connect Your Meetings website, "I love the thrill of having ideas and making them happen in real life. I love the shock that people get when they see me come out and I'm 27 years old, ex-military and a recent graduate." He learned time management, people skills, and how to handle multiple tasks at once. He said, "It's a really good career."

With more and more employees working remotely, a corporate event presents an opportunity for employees to come together face to face. It's a way to build morale, increase teamwork, generate ideas, and share knowledge. These events could be sales meetings, product launches, outward-bound-type teambuilding, corporate picnics, customer appreciation events, and employee appreciation events. In Las Vegas in 2013 alone, according to the Las Vegas Convention and Visitors Authority, there were more than twenty thousand events with nearly five million attendees. If you have a position as a corporate event planner, you can count on a steady stream of work.

Many think of event coordination as party planning. Birthdays, graduations, engagements, weddings, anniversaries, bar and bat mitzvahs, holidays, and family reunions are just some

Corporate events can serve as the bread-and-butter business for a successful event planner. These can range from training sessions to nighttime themed parties.

of the milestone events families celebrate. They benefit from having a professional event coordinator take charge of their special events. Some event planners specialize in social functions. They select the venue, come up with a theme and color scheme, and arrange for flowers, catering, music, invitations, and more.

Conventions and expositions are large-scale events that can take months and even years of proper planning. Many tend to take place every year. They may or may not include an exhibition or trade show space. For instance, Book Expo America, an annual event in New York City, offers exhibition space for publishers and others, who pay a fee to have a booth and promote their books. It attracts tens of thousands of industry professionals as well as consumers. Parking space, security, crowd management, and working with city officials are considerations for conventions and expos. Convention planners may work for a convention center or hall.

Closely related is the conference. A conference typically has a single theme, and speakers present about that theme. Conferences can be one-day or multiple-day events. Some industry association conferences can be quite large, involving tens of thousands of attendees, special events, and exhibit areas. Many rooms may need to be rented and set up for the event, and promotional materials may need to be created.

Association trade shows and annual conferences can be large events that could even span more than one venue and require transportation between multiple sites. Because attendance is not mandatory, good marketing is vital. The location of the event can vary from year to year, especially if it's a national or international association. Sometimes the term "conference" is used interchangeably with "convention" by the associations that hold them.

Charity balls and fund-raisers can provide glitz and glamour while raising money for good causes. These events may include auctions to help raise funds. The event coordinator may also need to get support from corporate sponsors. Charity balls and

Charity and fund-raising events often cater to wealthy people. Satisfying their needs for high-quality food and entertainment is a top priority for event coordinators.

fund-raisers can be gala events, and a gala may use a celebrity appearance as a way to attract potential donors. But fund-raisers can also be smaller events, such as when a church might need to raise money for a new roof. Associating yourself with a cause can be particularly meaningful and satisfying.

To plan a concert, a coordinator needs to hire performers, select the venue and dates, arrange for ticket sales, promote the event, and also consider security and transportation. It can be thrilling to meet musicians and then see them perform.

A special consideration for an art show is the hanging of the artwork. But like other events, a venue is necessary, plus a guest list, invitations, catering, and perhaps music.

Planning events for local, state, and federal government agencies can be a special niche. Learning government regulations for how to buy materials and booking hotels is important to being successful here.

There is a range of what the event industry calls "special events." These include festivals (food, wine, music, seasonal), fairs (art, book, town, Renaissance), dog shows, political rallies, theater productions (such as summer productions in the park), and sporting events (golf, marathons, triathlons, hockey games, football games, bike races, skating competitions, cancer walks, AIDS walks, diabetes walks). They occur in virtually every town, city, and state. Some may also be used as fund-raisers. Walks for cancer and other diseases take place to raise money to fund more research with the goal of finding a cure.

Special themed events require imagination, creativity, and a lot of hard work. But they can also be highly memorable and satisfying.

IT'S ALL POSSIBLE

You may start with small events or handling just a few aspects of a larger event. But, in the end, there are countless event planning opportunities, and you can get started right now. You can plan parties and school events. Volunteer with church or other community events.

Sandy Sloane planned her own wedding, her children's weddings, celebrations for family and friends, and lots of events in her school district. As a professional event planner, working with radio, television, cable, retail, and not-for-profit organizations, she created road races, golf tournaments, half-time shows during NFL games, concerts for five thousand to more than fifty thousand people, fashion shows, celebrity galas, product introductions, wine tastings, speaker seminars, walk-a-thons, read-a-thons, ski-a-thons, and trade shows. She also produced many south Florida events for the Walt Disney World Resort and was in charge of celebrities for the sixtienth annual Macy's Thanksgiving Day Parade.

chapter 2

LET'S GET THIS PARTY STARTED: SKILLS TO BUILD A SUCCESSFUL EVENT

Many of the skills needed to become a professional and successful event coordinator can show up early in life, even as early as grade school. By high school, those who eventually find careers in this field may receive compliments on their abilities to organize an event.

An event planning career requires lots of energy. Often long hours are involved, and an event coordinator may be standing for long periods of time. He or she may also have to pitch in and help with physical work, like setting up displays and moving tables and chairs.

THE COORDINATED, ORGANIZED EVENT COORDINATOR

Above all else, an event coordinator needs to be organized. While keeping track of the event at a high level, a coordinator must also pay attention to the smallest detail. Often, it's those details that can take an event off track. Computer skills can help the coordinator become and stay organized. Many successful event planners use computer software to keep track of their events, client contacts, vendor or supplier contacts, and budgets and costs. Being efficient goes hand in hand with good organization skills. Being mindful of budget and time is important. If you're constantly making to-do lists and checking off tasks you accomplish, that's good preparation for event planning.

Multitasking, an ability to handle many things at once, is a skill an event coordinator needs to have. At a single point in time, a coordinator may be wrapping up administrative details, such as billing, for one event, preparing a proposal for another, and researching venues for a third. The variety of tasks keeps the planner interested and motivated.

Sticklers for punctuality should have no problem managing deadlines. The timeline presented to clients and vendors must be executed as planned. A coordinator needs to manage not just his or her own time but also that of others.

Being organized and keeping a positive attitude are crucial to successful event coordination. Event planners need to be able to find client plans and vendor orders at a moment's notice.

LISTEN, SPEAK, AND WRITE

Good communication skills are also important. An event coordinator must be able to understand client needs fully. Then he or she must effectively communicate them to chefs, hotel staff, vendors, and others. Clients and vendors must always know the progress of their events. Event coordinators need to negotiate with vendors to get the best price and meet clients' goals. They need to be diplomatic yet firm when something goes wrong because something always will. A wedding cake may fall, a bride's dress may get caught in the limousine door, a venue may be double-booked, or the sound system may be broken—just to name a few examples.

Familiarity with e-mail and phone etiquette is a big plus. Planners often don't get the chance to meet with clients or vendors in person. When on the phone, they have to rely only on their voices to convey information. Their clients always need to feel that their best interests are the event coordinator's top priority.

THERE ARE NO PROBLEMS, ONLY CHALLENGES

Having a cool and calm head when problems arise is always useful. Handling customer complaints and resolving conflicts are vital skills for successful event coordination. Listening carefully to the complaint or problem and then applying diplomatic skills and creativity can help an event coordinator effectively fix the situation.

Event coordinators must be able to think on their feet. They have to quickly analyze options, especially during the event, and make decisions in the best interests of their client. An event planner makes dozens, if not more, decisions each day.

Flexibility, the ability to deal with problems as they arise, can help event coordinators deal with the unknown. They

A smile can be heard as well as seen. Clients and vendors can sense an event coordinator's mood even through the phone. They want to feel confident that the coordinator can solve their problems.

No Two Days Are Alike

While she was attending Virginia Tech as a hospitality and tourism management major, Christine Tambini learned that a career in event planning was not going to be dull. She told Lisa Plummer Savas on Connect Your Meetings, "The fact that every day is different is definitely true. That was something I knew and was excited about, because I don't like [to do] the same thing every day. You're not always sitting at the desk 9 to 5. You're out, you're traveling, you're meeting members and attendees."

need to prepare for the unexpected. The larger or more complex the event, the greater the possibility for issues to flare up. They need backup plans for their backup plans. There is no such thing as being too prepared.

Creative Juices Spark New Ideas

Creativity begins with a vision, an ability to see the big picture. An event planner needs to know the purpose of the event, how it should look and feel, and what experience he or she wants attendees or guests to leave with.

Creativity is an advantage for the savvy event coordinator. An eye for color and composition can help an event planner develop and suggest event themes that are fresh and innovative. They think beyond balloons and crepe paper. Even corporate events could have movie or theater themes or tropical adventure themes.

Onstage, Please

An event planner may be called on to give a speech. He or she may need to emcee an event, to stand before the entire group

Taking the lead is the event coordinator's job, even if that means stepping up to the microphone to address the audience.

and lead it. It's a good idea to participate in school plays or take acting classes to prepare. According to the National Institutes of Health, 74 percent of Americans have a fear of public speaking. The good news is that this fear is easily overcome with training and practice.

PASSPORT, ANYONE?

A willingness to travel and a sense of adventure can expand an event coordinator's career. For instance, more and more destination weddings and corporate meetings take place outside

A career in event coordination can be a great career choice for those who want extraordinary experiences. White-water rafting, for example, can be planned for a group outing.

North America. A corporate career could take the event planner to most of the United States and dozens of countries across the continents. While at these destinations, he or she might be able to sample local foods and see the local sights. Maybe kayaking on the Pacific Ocean. A helicopter ride through the Grand Canyon. Swimming with the dolphins in the Caribbean. Such experiences broaden the way a planner looks at the world while also giving clients memorable events.

Not everyone is willing to jump on a plane at a moment's notice. For those who prefer to stay closer to home, local events such as festivals, sporting events, and fund-raisers could be a good specialty area. Related jobs with companies that provide services to event coordinators, such as florists or decorators, may also offer local opportunities. A local convention or conference center can be a good choice, too.

TIME TO LEAD, TIME TO BE PART OF A TEAM

There are times when an event coordinator needs to lead and other times when he or she needs to be a team player. As a leader, the planner takes accountability for decisions and for budgets. He or she is responsible for pulling together all the activities of suppliers and others to create a single event. As a team player, the planner works together with caterers, venue staff, musicians, decorators, and others to create a spectacular event. The priority always is to satisfy the client, who is paying for the event.

WILLINGNESS TO LEARN

A commitment to learning and improving skills can only help. Always ask coworkers for help and seek advice of those with more experience. Event planners also subscribe to specialty magazines and newsletters and become familiar with special words used in the industry. Learning new trends helps them stay on top of their game.

A POSITIVE ATTITUDE LEADS TO A POSITIVE REPUTATION

Being social and friendly can benefit an event coordinator in a number of ways. Events are by their very nature social. Planners want attendees to have a good time, their clients to be satisfied with their service, and their suppliers to be eager to work with them again. They strive to show their enthusiasm. Overall, event planners want to establish a positive reputation. Each event offers a new opportunity to ask the client for a letter of reference. Word of mouth can recommend them for future events.

chapter 3

PLANNING FROM BEGINNING TO END

For event coordinators, activities follow a certain flow. Some tasks they perform on their own at their desks. Others take them to meetings with clients and vendors. Events and meetings could involve travel outside their local area or even the country.

PUNCTUAL, PROFESSIONAL, POSITIVE: THE FIRST MEETING

A planner first meets with the client. Being punctual and professional is important to making a positive first impression. The client needs to trust the planner with his or her special event and money. At this initial client meeting, the planner's goal is to find out exactly what the client needs. What is the reason for the special occasion? Are there expectations for a date and the number of hours or days for the event? What about location? An effective event coordinator takes careful notes and confirms what the client is saying. He or she also specifies what the event coordinator does and what the client does. For instance, if the event is a grand opening, the client may already have a guest list, including people from the media, such as radio and TV stations or newspapers, in mind. Then, the guest list would be the client's responsibility. Chances are that by the end of the first client meeting, the planner is already beginning to think about possible options.

THE THEME'S THE THING

A theme for the event is the thread that ties all the event activities together. It needs to be memorable. Some experts believe that an ability to present and deliver on a theme can make the difference between getting a client contract or not. The event coordinator needs to gain an understanding of the client's personality and interests. If the coordinator likes to take risks but the client does not, that theme of rock climbing or bungee jumping may not work.

WORKING WITH VENDORS

Once coordinators have an idea of what their clients need, they set out to speak with vendors that can supply them with the necessary services. Depending on the event, they may need to lock down dates, details, and costs with suppliers that provide catering, venue, hospitality staffing, lodging, decorating services, lighting, outdoor structures, entertainment, photography, videography, printing, floral design, promotional specialties (custom-designed items, such as T-shirts, coffee mugs, and pens), transportation, communication systems, signage (banners and other signs), and security. The event coordinator also needs to know the details of vendors' requirements for the event. For example, the lighting company may have specific power requirements that must be accommodated at the venue. Each vendor signs a contract with the event coordinator. The contract describes exactly what work or service the vendor will perform and at what price.

Event coordinators nurture relationships with both clients and vendors, such as bakeries. Planning goes much more smoothly when coordinators can rely on those with whom they have worked before.

Event coordinators who establish a specialty area have an opportunity to deepen vendor relationships. They may specifically want to work with the vendors they trust over and over again. For example, a professional bridal consultant may consistently rely on the same photographer or caterer. A coordinator

Visiting the site for an event helps the coordinator imagine how it will look. Often he or she will visit several sites for a single event and take notes on each.

who plans events all over the world may decide to work with a production company—a company that manages staging, lighting, sound, and perhaps entertainment—with whom he or she has had success before. When planners work with a vendor they know, they have a better idea of what they can expect from them. They know how well the vendor meets deadlines. They know how to communicate best with the vendor. They can anticipate any problems. And, the vendor has a better idea of how it can meet the planner's requirements and demands. A good relationship with a vendor can make an event flow much more smoothly for everyone involved.

A VISIT TO THE SITE

An event planner will likely have a few sites in mind for the event. A visit to each of these sites is critical. The event coordinator needs to see the space personally and have a checklist on hand to help determine the site's suitability for the event. The meeting space must match the needs of the event, the client, and the guests. If planning an event for senior citizens, restrooms and other facilities need to be close to the meeting space. Special accommodations, including food preparation to meet certain dietary restrictions, may be also necessary. Photos of the sites can be presented to the client for final approval.

SEALING THE DEAL: CLIENT APPROVAL FOR THE EVENT

All the information gathered from the client and vendors goes into a document called a proposal. It outlines the event coordinator's approach to the event. Sealing the deal with signatures on a contract, the client typically pays a deposit—a percentage of the overall cost—at this point, so the event coordinator can get started.

The Elements of an Event Planning Proposal

A proposal can be broad or very detailed. It may also list options so the client can decide what's best. An event planner may be able to imagine how an event will look. But often a client cannot. Details can be spelled out in the proposal so the client can see what the planner sees. After all, clients come to planners for their expertise. Client approval of the proposal, which requires a signature, is the starting point for the formal process of coordinating the event.

A typical proposal includes the following elements:

Statement of the event's objective
A profile of the guest list
    Who will be attending?
    Is this a private or public event?
    Is the number of attendees open or limited to a specific number?
Specifics of the event
    Time
    Place
    Budget
Description and theme
    Décor
    Photos that present the planner's visual ideas
Entertainment
    Selections for music or other performers
Food and beverage
Other services required
    Invitations
    Goodie bags
    Signs

Timeline
A depiction of planning activities by day, week, and/or month—from the initial client meeting to the actual event and follow-up activities after the event
Cost estimates
Including the event coordinator's time
Event measurement
How will success of the event be measured?
Evaluation cards for a corporate event
Press coverage for a product launch or grand opening
Amount of money raised for a charity

The timeline is particularly critical. This is how the event planner keeps the project on track. The timeline can be shared with the vendors so everyone is on the same page and is committed to the same goals.

Another item related to time is a detailed plan for the event itself. This could be in the form of an agenda or schedule that shows which speakers present at which times and in which rooms, when there will be breaks, when and where there will be social events, and more.

MAKING THINGS HAPPEN: THE PRODUCTION SCHEDULE

Thoughtful planning right from the beginning can smooth the coordinating process. Event planners use a timeline, also called a production schedule, to record all the steps and activities needed for the event. The timeline includes set up for the event and take down. For example, a conference in a large hall or convention center requires many tasks to make sure everything is in place for its opening. Once the conference is over, all the exhibits must be taken apart, all the signs have to be taken down, and all extra promotional materials need to be discarded.

On the day of an event, every detail must be checked and double-checked, including floral arrangements.

To be ready for the event, legal permissions, such as licenses or permits, may be necessary. Speakers for a conference may need transportation. Centerpieces may need to be created and delivered. The production schedule includes all preparations, a complete vendor list, delivery schedules, setup, and takedown.

As the day of the event nears, the planner arranges for a walk-through at the venue as a rehearsal for the event. The event coordinator needs to make sure everything from sound systems to lighting to table settings will work according to plan. Meetings with vendors onsite are usually necessary to help ensure success.

THE BIG DAY ARRIVES

Event coordinators are typically onsite during their events, making sure all the moving parts come together. They want every part of the event to run smoothly for their clients, guests, vendors, and themselves. If problems arise, they must make quick decisions to resolve them. They prepare for a long day or several long days,

Planning for celebrity fund-raisers, such as this one for a children's charity attended by actress Brooke Shields and her daughter, can help raise awareness of important causes through media attention.

depending on the duration of the events. The event day is a workday. They make sure the food is delivered on time, the entertainment isn't too loud, and no one becomes unruly.

But they also find a moment or two to stand back and witness the great events they created, all those days, weeks, and months of hard work finally realized. They watch the smiles of couples dancing, they hear the claps of the audience, or they see a standing ovation when a great speaker finishes a presentation.

To many event planners, customer satisfaction is the most important goal. For Sandy Sloane, contributing to a cause has been her best moment as an event planner. While she was marketing director for a top radio station in New York City, the AIDS epidemic was at its height. Sloane wanted to help because so many people around her got sick and died from the disease. She created an annual radiothon to raise money for several AIDS organizations. She pulled in major celebrities, including Donald Trump, Patrick Swayze, Brooke Shields, and dozens more. They helped to answer the phones. She also lined up musical groups to entertain.

The radio show was live, and many local businesses donated food and drinks for the volunteers. Sloane said, "We raised over $500,000 from donations, received local, national, and international press, made money for the radio station, and best of all, raised awareness about AIDS throughout New York by having educational seminars for school children at the night club venue that hosted the 24 hour event." The radio station became known as "the station that cares."

WRAPPING IT ALL UP

Just because the event itself is over doesn't mean the event coordinator's job is done. The coordinator must check all the vendors' bills to make sure billing is correct and then must pay the vendors. Evaluations need to be completed to determine whether the event was a success. Will attendees return next year? Increasingly, clients view events as a way to drive business. Did the event bring in money? Planners must report results to their clients.

A DAY IN THE LIFE OF AN EVENT COORDINATOR

No event is really typical, so each day for an event planner can be unique. But here's a look at one day for an event planner:

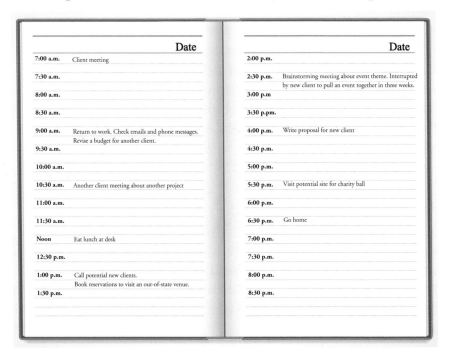

		Date
7:00 a.m.	Client meeting	
7:30 a.m.		
8:00 a.m.		
8:30 a.m.		
9:00 a.m.	Return to work. Check emails and phone messages. Revise a budget for another client.	
9:30 a.m.		
10:00 a.m.		
10:30 a.m.	Another client meeting about another project	
11:00 a.m.		
11:30 a.m.		
Noon	Eat lunch at desk	
12:30 p.m.		
1:00 p.m.	Call potential new clients. Book reservations to visit an out-of-state venue.	
1:30 p.m.		

		Date
2:00 p.m.		
2:30 p.m.	Brainstorming meeting about event theme. Interrupted by new client to pull an event together in three weeks.	
3:00 p.m		
3:30 p.pm.		
4:00 p.m.	Write proposal for new client	
4:30 p.m.		
5:00 p.m.		
5:30 p.m.	Visit potential site for charity ball	
6:00 p.m.		
6:30 p.m.	Go home	
7:00 p.m.		
7:30 p.m.		
8:00 p.m.		
8:30 p.m.		

A typical day could involve between three to six meetings, phone calls, deadlines for proposals, creating layouts of events, fielding phone calls, handling budget issues, and more. At busy times of the year, an event planner could work sixty or more hours a week.

chapter 4

PREPARING FOR AN EVENT COORDINATION CAREER

In the past, many event coordinators said they stumbled upon their careers. But today, young people often know they want to be event planners. They know that clients want to use meetings and events to drive business, educate, and celebrate special occasions. Today's event coordinators want to be prepared to meet challenges head on. The best preparation is a combination of hands-on experience and formal education. That preparation can begin when the aspiring event planner is still in school.

VOLUNTEERING COUNTS

Event planners agree that volunteering for activities can help build a résumé. Volunteering provides experience before committing to a full-time career. It also puts future event planners in places where they can meet people who may become important contacts. Close to home, schools and communities may need volunteers to help organize events. Schools may need help with programs for parents, dances, plays, concerts, talent shows, and fund-raisers. Communities may need help with a holiday parade, street festival, art show featuring local artists, summer programs for younger children, and more. Local museums, art

Summer jobs, like camp counselor, can build skills for group organization and activities planning. When included on a résumé, they can help a job candidate for event coordination stand out.

galleries, social service organizations, and hospitals may also need assistance with their events. Even helping out at a community theater can teach set design and lighting. A volunteer commitment should last for at least six months.

JOBS ON THE SIDE

Many students work after school and on weekends. Serving as wait staff or host in a restaurant or a receptionist in an office and even delivering pizza involve working with all kinds of people. Anyone with this type of experience gains valuable insights that can be useful later in event coordination. Seek opportunities at local hotels, florists, and catering companies. Learning how these places operate makes it that much easier for event planners when they have to work with them later.

TAKING INTERESTS AND HOBBIES TO THE NEXT LEVEL

While growing up, many event coordinators liked to bake or cook. Some had a passion for fashion or enjoyed art or music. Their friends came to them to create their party invitations and favors. These interests led them to a career in event coordination. Aspiring event planners can make more time to further develop these interests. If they like to cook, they could offer to cater an event. If people compliment them on the way they dress, they could help dress friends for a sweet 16 birthday party or other celebration.

CLASSES NOW PAY OFF LATER

Students in a traditional high school or vocational school have opportunities to develop themselves for a career in event coordination. A course in marketing gives an idea of how events are

An interest in music or art can help a coordinator choose suitable music or décor for an event. It can also impress a potential employer.

part of a corporation's or organization's plan to drive business. A business class can teach about finances and profitability and the ways potential clients and employers will be looking at events. A public speaking class can help build confidence for interviews and to address small and large groups of people. Theater is a great way not only to improve stage presence but also to learn important backstage activities, such as lighting, props, set design, and special effects. An art class can give an appreciation for composition and color. A music appreciation class can help further refine listening skills and broaden knowledge of music. As an event planner, communication skills need to be top notch, so a class in writing and in interpersonal communications can be helpful. Finally, a class in technology can help polish computer skills to perfect organizational abilities.

GETTING THE COLLEGE DEGREE

While a college degree is not necessary to become an event coordinator, having a degree can give planners a competitive advantage. It means they'll be better prepared and will have gone through rigorous training. With the number of meetings and events on the rise, the more credentials they have, the easier it can be for them to find a full-time position.

An associate's degree in meeting and event planning, or a similarly named major, is typically the result of a two-year program and provides more specialized education in event

COLLEGE CERTIFICATION IN ONE YEAR

Some community colleges offer a one-year (thirty credit) certificate program in event planning. For example, at Raritan Valley Community College in New Jersey, students can get an event planning/meeting management certificate after completing course work in the following classes:

English composition
  • Interpersonal communication
  • Business, marketing

(continued on the next page)

(continued from the previous page)

- Event planning/meeting management
- Speech
- Business law
- Public relations
- Computer literacy
- Event production
- Communication/speech

planning. Getting an associate's degree can give a solid, practical foundation and introduce the breadth of activities involved in event planning.

In the event production course, students produce an event, manage its budget and timeline, create menus and advertising, and handle all tasks normally associated with producing an event. There is also a cooperative option where students work in the field actually planning events and managing meetings.

Some colleges and universities offer four-year bachelor's degree programs in hospitality where students can minor in meetings and event planning. These programs, which may bear the name "event marketing," "hospitality management," "tourism management," or "hotel management," typically require courses in a variety of areas, including business, management, finance, law, writing, convention planning, and festival and event management. Indiana University in Bloomington, Indiana, for instance, offers a bachelor of science (BS) degree in recreation, with a major in tourism, hospitality, and event management. The program requires 320 hours of practical field experience and an internship. The more students combine course work with practical experience, the better. This gives them the best of both worlds and helps them develop a very impressive résumé. Some planners go beyond the bachelor's degree to pursue an advanced degree at the master's level.

INTERNSHIPS AND EXTERNSHIPS

As event planning as a career becomes increasingly popular, experience can help set an aspiring coordinator apart from others who want the same job. Internships can make the difference. A savvy person could contact local companies and ask to serve as an unpaid intern for three months.

Some educational programs offer or require internships, such as working in a local restaurant or campus food service. Such internships may or may not count for college credit and may or may not be paid.

Another possibility is an externship. An externship is a very brief introduction to a career and usually lasts from one week to just a few months. It's typically an unpaid position, but it could give valuable insights into event planning. It could also provide important contacts for when an aspiring coordinator is ready to find a full-time position.

GETTING CERTIFIED THROUGH UNIVERSITIES AND CONTINUING EDUCATION PROGRAMS

Some universities offer certification programs. The University of Massachusetts, for instance, offers a fifteen-credit online program where students take classes in hospitality personnel management; special events management; meeting, convention, and exposition management; food service management; and convention sales management.

New York University's School of Continuing and Professional Studies in New York City offers a certificate in conference and meeting management, requiring students to complete seven courses. Five are specifically required: meeting and conference management, catering for meetings and events, budgeting and financial management for meeting managers, marketing and revenue strategies for meeting planners, and use of current technologies in the meeting industry. In addition, students choose two electives from courses in negotiation, design and décor, managing special event vendors, special events management, and wedding planning.

George Washington University in Washington, D.C., also offers a certificate program in event management. Here, students complete four required courses and three electives, plus one hundred hours of event management practical experience. Students develop an event portfolio that documents an actual event the student has planned from beginning to end.

Getting Certified Through Event Planning Organizations

In the event planning world, certain certifications designate a planner as a professional and are, therefore, useful for career advancement. Industry organizations grant these certifications. Many employers and

clients want to hire a planner who has undergone a certification program. To earn certification typically requires at least three years' experience plus education.

The best-known credential is the certified meeting professional (CMP), a certification granted by the Convention

Schools like New York University offer continuing education classes and often certification in event planning or coordination.

Industry Council. Planners can also become certified special events professionals (CSEPs). The International Special Events Society grants this credential. Meeting Professionals International offers the Certificate in Meeting Management (CMM), another important designation. Those interested in working with government organizations may want to earn the certified government meeting professional (CGMP) credential offered by the Society of Government Meeting Professionals. To qualify, an applicant must have worked as a meeting planner for at least one year, among other requirements.

MANY OPTIONS, MANY OPPORTUNITIES

Event coordinators can choose from a number of paths to get started in their careers. They can opt for a certificate they earn online or get a bachelor's degree and gain hours of hands-on experience through internships. According to the U.S. Bureau of Labor Statistics, job opportunities are best for event planners with a bachelor's degree in hospitality management. Attending a university in a state or city that tends to attract large numbers of tourists can offer unique opportunities for internships and professional contacts. Educational opportunities are increasing, too. As the need for more event planners develops, more college and universities are offering programs.

In the world of event coordination, planners never stop learning. They meet new people and learn on the job every day.

chapter 5

FROM FIRST PLANNING JOB TO EVENT COORDINATION CAREER

I n entry-level, full-time positions, event coordinators may be working with small events. As they learn more and gain more experience, they can advance to performing multiple tasks for a single event or take on the challenge of a larger event.

According to the U.S. Bureau of Labor Statistics, event planners can get a greater opportunity to learn more quickly if they take a job at a small organization. With less staff, the smaller organization offers a greater variety of activities to handle.

The first few years in event coordination may feel like an army boot camp. There's much to learn and not much time available. But for those willing to jump in and learn from every experience, these years can be some of the most rewarding. They can also strengthen the commitment to the industry.

A MIX OF SKILLS AND REQUIREMENTS

Not all jobs are created equal, and aspiring planners give themselves the best chance for success by thinking about the type of job that matches their skills and personality. For instance, a job with a corporation to plan its events would be very different from a position with a convention hall. The size of events will vary, as will their time commitments. If event coordination job seekers prefer more nights at home, they are better matches for positions at corporations, museums, universities, and hospitals. However, even these employers may require long hours spilling over into evenings and weekends.

HIT THE GROUND RUNNING

Donte Clavo did not have much experience when he faced the challenge of planning a conference for Thurgood Marshall College Fund within two months. But he had to make it work. Everything seemed to be happening all at the same time: the food, the sleeping arrangements, people who were supposed to come but didn't. He told Lisa Plummer Savas, "I was up all night for five days setting up, breaking down, working with production teams and doing the expo. I was putting out fires, working with a team I'd just met and trying to impress my company. It was intense. I think I paid all of my dues at one time."

But this experience helped him deal with the far greater challenge of setting up an event in New York City just as Super Storm Sandy was about to hit in October 2012. He learned the importance of preparing for emergencies.

CREATING THE RÉSUMÉ

An aspiring event planner's résumé should highlight any related experience: customer service, catering, restaurant positions, fund-raising, event planning, decorating, public relations, or marketing. For instance, someone who worked on a fund-raiser should mention the event and describe the activities and the

A résumé offers a job candidate the opportunity to highlight skills and experiences that demonstrate event planning promise.

results he or she achieved. The résumé should certainly include any internships or practical experience gained during a degree or certificate program. It should also provide details about classes and activities in public speaking, business, marketing, writing, and theater.

A TYPICAL JOB DESCRIPTION FOR AN ENTRY-LEVEL POSITION

Entry-Level Planning and Event Coordinator

Seeking a candidate for an entry-level planning and event coordinator for one of the leading event promotions and event planning firms in the country. We are looking for an innovative, team-oriented individual who enjoys working with others and maintaining relationships with prestigious clientele. This position will be working hands-on with private promotions, advertising, and special events designed and coordinated by the firm.

The main focus of this position is to promote our clients' brand names by developing and supporting field marketing programs. You will work closely with other event marketing specialists and corporate marketing and sales organizations to support sales activities (shows, events, campaigns, etc.) and utilize your marketing expertise to help develop and execute marketing programs that will increase demand and drive revenue.

Primary duties:
- Impact sales results by developing, supporting, and executing field marketing and segment activities
- Execute marketing campaigns and plan events depending on expertise
- Work with various corporate/field marketing managers to determine appropriate customized programs and strategies for various market segments
- Publicize events and work with account development to raise awareness and drive high levels of attendance and participation by targeted audience

Qualifications:
- Outstanding communication skills both verbal and written
- Able to prioritize and work independently with minimal supervision
- Able to work effectively in a team environment
- College degree
- Flexible availability; able to work some weekends
- No experience is necessary; this is an entry-level position

Fast Forward: Advancing a Career in Event Coordination

There is a wide variety of jobs available to a new event coordinator. These include event assistant, meeting planner, event planner or coordinator, account manager, and trade show manager.

Most people typically stay in entry-level jobs from one to three years. During these initial years, as planners gain confidence and begin to master certain tasks, it's always a good idea to volunteer for greater responsibilities. The level of skill and determination, and whether peers respect them can make the difference between planners' advancing and staying in the same or similar position. Coordinators can also increase their level of education. For example, a planner with a two-year degree might decide to pursue professional certification or decide to go for a bachelor's degree online or at a local university.

As event coordinators progress, they could assume more duties or gain experience in a different specialty area. For example, planners could first work as event specialists, where they handle logistics. They could move to roles as project

Truly understanding a client's needs and helping the client make the best possible choices can help build a successful event coordinator career.

coordinators where they arrange for speakers and other event programming. Then they could take on positions as event managers, responsible for all aspects of events, perhaps supervising the work of others.

The more experience coordinators gain, the more opportunity they have to work directly with clients. Beyond that, with a foundation of extensive experience, they could decide to branch out on their own. They could become independent consultants, executive directors of an association, or meeting and exhibits or tradeshow directors for corporations.

DEVELOPING A PORTFOLIO

Beginning with a first project, an event coordinator develops a visual portfolio of the events he or she has handled. Such a portfolio, a kind of a scrapbook, can be useful in meetings with prospective employers and clients. This way they can see the kind of work the planner has done before. When interviewing for a first job, an applicant can include in his or her portfolio photos from events planned as an intern, volunteer, or student.

Attending professional events is one important way an event planner continues to learn the coordination business.

STAYING CONNECTED

While working, event coordinators find it useful to expand their network of contacts in the industry. One way they do this is through professional event planning organizations. Membership in one or more of the associations gives access to more experienced professionals, best practices in the industry, additional training opportunities, and in some cases, certification programs. Some planners make a commitment to attending at least one event industry conference a year. The International Special Events Society holds a three-day conference annually called Eventworld. Primedia Business Exhibitions produces a similar event known as the Special Event every January.

chapter 6

MEETING THE FUTURE THROUGH SOCIAL MEDIA

The future of events is changing and so is the role of the event planner. Social media and mobile apps are making a big hit in the industry. Event coordinators are using social media—Facebook, LinkedIn, Twitter, Pinterest, and YouTube, among others—to increase engagement, build event loyalty, and promote the event before, during, and after it takes place. Developing a social media strategy is now a must for an event; it's a critical ingredient to increasing event registrations. The event planner must think about the goals for using social media. He or she could want to increase attendance, educate the potential audience, bring in new sponsors, or promote a new product. Research may be required among the social media sites to understand just where conversations are taking place.

SOCIAL MEDIA ENHANCE THE ATTENDEE EXPERIENCE

Bear in mind, social media is also a two-way street. Increasingly, it's about inspiring conversation, not just getting "hits." When someone posts, the event coordinator needs to respond to keep the conversation going. Closely listening to and monitoring conversations helps the event coordinator stay current and

Today's coordinators rely on social media, such as LinkedIn, to help publicize their events both before and after they take place.

involved. Paying attention to keywords, phrases, and topics and including them in messages can increase their relevance to the audience.

In general, LinkedIn is best used for professional events such as business conferences and meetings, while Facebook is best for personal events such as festivals, social functions, public fund-raisers, and sporting events.

AMAZING MEDIA: USING SOCIAL MEDIA BEFORE AN EVENT

Before social media, an event planner could announce the event through a well-crafted press release and media contacts. Now, that's just not enough. Event planners are encouraged to use social media throughout the registration process. There are several positive aspects to this. Before the meeting, the event planner can use social media to increase registrations. It's important to reach out through social media, going to the "watering hole" where potential attendees gather. For instance, an association might host its own LinkedIn group. An announcement about an event to that group could attract new registrants who might not have otherwise known about the event.

Through social media, attendees can network with each other even before the event happens. They can set up meetings, share their interests, and expand their list of contacts.

Word-of-mouth promotion can help save money. Event coordinators may still use traditional approaches of printed promotional brochures, invitations, and/or advertising, but using social media before an event is a cost-effective method to get the word out there about their event.

The event coordinator can use social media to create buzz and excitement about the event, share the growing number of registrants, give a sneak peek into content, share photos, use quotes from influential people, and more. Some event planners create contests, inviting registrants to share that they've registered with the goal of bringing in even more people. It's all part of creating enthusiasm for the event. Others create ready-made Twitter messages that registrants can easily share through their own Twitter accounts.

RIGHT IN THE ACTION: USING SOCIAL MEDIA DURING AN EVENT

While at an event, attendees scramble from session to session and deal with interruptions from their electronic devices. Instead of turning off those devices, they can use them in the context of the event. They can tweet or send Facebook messages about the event. The host of the conference can do this, too, all arranged and anticipated by the tech-savvy event planner, who knows exactly how to harness the power of social media.

From a strategic perspective, an event coordinator can work together with speakers, industry leaders, bloggers, the press, sponsors, and exhibitors to generate buzz throughout the course of the event. Some planners include social media in speakers' contracts, gaining an upfront commitment to speaker help and support for promoting the event.

Feedback from the previous year's event could identify potential pain points for the attendees. Maybe there were complaints about long registration lines or too few restrooms. An event coordinator could use social media to let attendees know these problems have been resolved and highlight other improvements. The goal is always to create a positive experience so attendees return each year.

Investments in technology can help the event coordinator stay efficient, effective, and always in touch with clients and vendors.

At some conferences, attendees are encouraged to tweet throughout the event. Event planners monitor the tweets and publicly thank attendees for them, and some hold contests such as the best tweets of the day or the conference.

KEEP THE MOMENTUM: USING SOCIAL MEDIA AFTER AN EVENT

Following an event, coordinators can use social media to keep registrants coming back year after year. Announcing results from the meeting, sharing anecdotes from attendees and educational content from speakers, and posting photos and videos can keep enthusiasm fresh for the next meeting. The content will always be available to those seeking information. And now it will be searchable and accessible through the Web. It's a cost-effective way to maintain and even enlarge a community after an event. Attendees can also give the event coordinator immediate feedback through social media.

MOBILE APPS: THE NEW DIGITAL JOURNAL FOR EVENTS

CrowdCompass, a Portland, Oregon, event mobile app developer for professional events, reports that the average smartphone user has sixty-five apps on his or her phone and uses fifteen apps in a given week. That presents an opportunity to the event coordinator, who can create a specific app for an event and work to make this app one of the fifteen used. Courtney Young, a spokesperson for the National Council for Community Behavioral Healthcare in Washington, D.C., told CrowdCompass, "With more than 3,000 people at our conference, we needed a fast way to communicate updates and increase engagement. Our mobile app was a big hit. More than

80 percent downloaded it and our members now see us as ahead of the curve."

A mobile app can be used to share changes in the agenda, remind attendees of upcoming events with video previews, share highlights of speaker presentations, and more. It can be a digital journal for the event. After the event, the mobile app can remind attendees of the people they met and want to stay in touch with and the presentations that gave them breakthrough ideas, and it can provide a way to keep the conversation going.

A study conducted by the Center for Exhibition Industry Research (CEIR) reported that 73 percent of younger participants create a "must see" list of exhibitors before attending a conference. A mobile app lets attendees prepare their itineraries in advance, because once they arrive, it's a scramble for time.

VIRTUAL EVENTS ON THE RISE

Research firm Market Research Media, Inc. estimates that virtual events, including conferences and trade shows using the Internet and social media, will grow 56 percent through 2018. Virtual events are attractive because they can reach wide audiences and attract more attendees than ever. Nevertheless, they still need event coordinators to develop and execute plans for their success. Virtual event planners may help determine a location for events and educational conferences, help manage meetings, and offer support for online virtual functions. They may also help with graphic design and creating avatars, the icons used to represent people in virtual worlds.

According to the U.S. Bureau of Labor Statistics, event planning job applicants with experience in social media and virtual meeting software should have an advantage over those who don't.

Successful event coordinators study culinary, entertainment, and decorating trends to give their clients the best guidance.

CURRENT TRENDS AND CHANGING ROLES

Beyond social media and mobile apps, other trends are predicted to affect the industry, too. Event attendees now want more natural light and open spaces. They want more opportunity to network with each other and to interact with speakers. They request interactive content and even gaming.

From a culinary perspective, the demand for organic food is on the rise. That can increase the cost of food for an event.

Event coordinators are always ready to travel to visit sites, meet with clients and vendors, and attend the events themselves.

Both venues and clients continue to look for value. They want to drive business, and it's the event coordinator's role to deliver it. Also, the way an event is evaluated is changing. While there's still an eye on financial results for some and number of attendees for others, the amount of conversation about the event provides a whole new category of measurement.

Increasingly, organizations are looking to hold their meetings in other countries. That means the event planner must have an up-to-date passport and be ready to travel. Knowledge of other languages is a definite plus.

COMPETITION AND ECONOMY SHAPE THE JOB MARKET

Although the number of event planning jobs is expected to increase, the U.S. Bureau of Labor Statistics expects strong competition for these jobs. Those who have a bachelor's degree in hospitality or tourism management may have better chances at finding work, as may those who hold a credential such as a certified meeting professional (CMP). Also, opportunities for corporate event planners may rise and fall depending on the economy. If the economy faces a downturn, corporations may need to cut meeting budgets. However, event coordinators in the health care industry may fare better. Medical professionals are often required to attend association meetings and conferences to maintain their licenses.

THE BOTTOM LINE

An event coordinator's career will face challenges, whether it's the economy, technology, or social opinions. But it's a fast-growing industry with opportunity to make people happy and continually learn.

glossary

certificate Shows completion of an educational program. It is not, however, the same as certification.

certification Proof that one has met special qualifications in a field of study.

conference An official assembly of association members or a large gathering of people typically to confer, discuss, and share research.

convention An official assembly or a large gathering of people who share common interests.

crowd management A set of strategies and tactics to help protect attendees at public events, especially when a large number of attendees is expected, such as at a concert or exposition.

culinary Related to the art of cooking.

exhibition A public display, such as exhibitor booths at an association conference or trade show.

exposition A large-scale public exhibition similar to a trade show or fair; the name can be shortened to "expo."

externship Similar to an internship but usually lasting between one week and three months; it gives an introduction to a career or job.

function Another name for an event or social activity.

fund-raiser An event usually hosted by an association or school to raise money.

gala A festive occasion that is typically formal.

internship A paid or unpaid opportunity to gain practical, hands-on experience in a professional field.

media The press and television and radio reporters; also includes bloggers.

press release A written announcement of an event to generate interest. It is released to the media with the goal of getting the word out there.

production The process of putting on an event. It includes staging, lighting, sound, and set design.

proposal A document an event planner prepares that details the event. It includes a timeline and a budget.

staging The process of setting up an event, much like getting a stage ready for a performance.

tent A portable structure used outdoors and often made of cloth and held up by poles, sometimes quite large, specifically installed to house an event.

venue The location of an event, for instance, a convention center or a hotel ballroom.

for more information

Canadian Association of Exposition Management (CAEM)
160 Tycos Drive
Suite 2219
Box 218
Toronto, ON M6B 1W8
Canada
(866) 441-9377
Website: http://www.caem.ca
Formed in the 1970s, the Canadian Association of Exposition
    Management is Canada's national association for profes-
    sionals who produce, manage, and plan trade shows and
    other events.

Canadian Society of Professional Event Planners (CanSPEP)
312 Oakwood Court
Newmarket, ON L3Y 3C8
Canada
(866) 467-2299
Website: http://canspep.ca
The Canadian Society of Professional Event Planners,
    founded in 1996, serves event planners who run their own
    businesses. Its members have clients in the corporate,
    association, government, and not-for-profit markets.

Center for Exhibition Industry Research (CEIR)
12700 Park Central Drive
Suite 308
Dallas, TX 75251
(972) 687-9242
Website: http://www.ceir.org

The Center for Exhibition Industry Research is a not-for-
profit organization that conducts research for the
exhibition industry. It helps planners meet client needs
and improve their business performance.

Convention Industry Council (CIC)
700 N. Fairfax Street
Suite 510
Alexandria, VA 22314
(571) 527-3116
Website: http://www.conventionindustry.org
The Convention Industry Council provides a forum for its
member organizations to exchange information on
global trends and topics and share best practices.
It covers the meetings, conventions, exhibitions,
and events industry and grants the certified meeting
professional (CMP) credential.

George Washington University
Event Management Certificate Program
Business Certificate Programs
11 South Angell Street
P.O. Box 169
Providence, RI 02906
(877) 498-4477
Website: http://gwueventmanagement.augusoft.net/index
.cfm?fuseaction=1065&
George Washington University offers an event management
certificate program that includes many hours of hands-on
experience through fieldwork and an internship.

International Festivals and Events Association (IFEA)
2603 W. Eastover Terrace
Boise, ID 83706

(208) 433-0950
Website: http://www.ifea.com
Originally founded in 1956 and named the Festival Manager's
    Association, the International Festivals and Events
    Association serves event and festival professionals with
    partners and affiliates all over the world.

International Special Events Society (ISES)
330 N. Wabash Avenue
Chicago, IL 60611
(800) 688-4737
Website: http://www.ises.com
The International Special Events Society promotes education
    and ethical conduct for event and meeting professionals. It
    was founded in 1987 and grants the certified special event
    professional (CSEP) designation.

Meetings Professionals International (MPI)
3030 Lyndon B. Johnson Freeway
Suite 1700
Dallas, TX 75234
(972) 702-3000
Website: http://www.mpiweb.org
Meetings Professionals International was founded in 1972
    and has more than twenty thousand members around the
    globe. It provides members with professional development
    opportunities, including the Certificate in Meeting
    Management (CMM).

Professional Convention Management Association (PCMA)
35 East Wacker Drive
Suite 500
Chicago, IL 60601
(877) 827-7262

Website: http://www.pcma.org

The Professional Convention Management Association is a professional organization for meeting planners, suppliers, and students. It has more than six thousand members worldwide, with chapters in the United States, Canada, and Mexico.

UMassOnline
333 South Street
Suite 400
Shrewsbury, MA 01545
(877) 698-6277
Website: http://www.umassonline.net/degrees/online
     -certificate-event-management

The University of Massachusetts offers an online certificate program in meeting and event management through UMassOnline.

WEBSITES

Because of the changing nature of Internet links, Rosen Publishing has developed an online list of websites related to the subject of this book. This site is updated regularly. Please use this link to access the list:

http://www.rosenlinks.com/ECAR/Event

for further reading

Abraham, Richard. *Mr. Shmooze: The Art and Science of Selling Through Relationships.* New York, NY: Wiley, 2010.

Allen, Judy. *Confessions of an Event Planner.* New York, NY: Wiley, 2009.

Allen, Judy. *Event Planning Ethics and Etiquette.* New York, NY: Wiley, 2010.

Chiu, Lisa. *Event Planners: Stories from People Who've Done It.* 101 Publishing, 2012. Kindle edition.

Devitt, Dianne Budion. *What Color Is Your Event: The Art of Bringing People Together.* Riverdale, NY: DnD Group, Inc., 2010.

Fisher, Roger, William L. Ury, and Bruce Patton. *Getting to Yes: Negotiating Agreement Without Giving In.* Revised ed. New York, NY: Penguin, 2011.

Gilbert, Jennifer. *I Never Promised You a Goodie Bag.* New York, NY: Harper, 2012.

Goldblatt, Joe. *Special Events: Creating and Sustaining a New World for Celebration.* New York, NY: Wiley, 2014.

Kabani, Shama Hyder. *The Zen of Social Media Marketing: An Easier Way to Build Credibility, Generate Buzz, and Increase Revenue.* Third ed. Dallas, TX: BenBella, 2013.

Malouf, Lena. *Events Exposed: Managing and Designing Special Events.* New York, NY: Wiley, 2012.

Novak, David. *Taking People with You: The Only Way to Make Big Things Happen.* New York, NY: Portfolio/Penguin, 2012.

Oppenheim, Silvia. *The Best Book on Event Planning Careers.* San Francisco, CA: Hyperink, 2011.

Preston, C.A. *Event Marketing: How to Successfully Promote Events, Festivals, Conventions, and Expositions.* New York, NY: Wiley, 2012.

Professional Convention Management. *Professional Meeting Management: Comprehensive Strategies for Meetings, Conventions and Events.* Dubuque, IA: Kendall Hunt, 2013.

Saget, Allison. *The Event Marketing Handbook.* CreateSpace, 2012.

Smith, Martin P. *The New Exhibitor.* Troy, OH: MCG Family Corporation, 2011.

Stark, David. *The Art of the Party.* New York, NY: Monacelli Press, 2013.

bibliography

Allen, Judy. *Event Planning: The Ultimate Guide to Successful Meetings, Corporate Events, Fundraising Galas, Conferences, Conventions, Incentives and Other Special Events.* New York, NY: Wiley, 2000.

Bureau of Labor Statistics, U.S. Department of Labor. *Occupational Outlook Handbook, 2012-13 Edition.* "Meeting, Convention, and Event Planners." Retrieved January 17, 2014 (http://www.bls.gov/ooh/business-and-financial/meeting-convention-and-event-planners.htm).

Bureau of Labor Statistics, U.S. Department of Labor. "Occupational Employment and Wages, May 2012: Meeting, Convention, and Event Planners." Retrieved January 17, 2014 (http://www.bls.gov/oes/current/oes131121.htm#(1)).

Camenson, Blythe. *Opportunities in Event Planning.* New York, NY: VGM Career Books/McGraw-Hill, 2003.

Castro, Kimberly. "Best Business Jobs: Meeting, Convention & Event Planner." Retrieved January 5, 2014 (http://money.usnews.com/careers/best-jobs/meeting-convention-and-event-planner).

Coastal Communications Corporation. *Association & Convention Facilities Magazine.* Retrieved March 4, 2014 (http://www.themeetingmagazines.com/association-conventions-facilities).

Coastal Communications Corporation. *Corporate & Incentive Travel Magazine.* Retrieved March 4, 2014 (http://www.themeetingmagazines.com/corporate-incentive-travel).

Collinson Meetings and Events. *Connect Magazine.* Retrieved March 4, 2014 (http://www.connectyourmeetings.com).

Craven, Robin E., and Lynn Johnson Golabowski. *The Complete Idiot's Guide to Meeting and Event Planning.* Second ed. New York, NY: Alpha/Penguin, 2004.

Evans, Sirena. *Become an Event Planner: The Three Necessary Steps to Begin Your Event Planning Career.* Retrieved January 2014 (http://www.careers-in-event-planning.com).

Friedmann, Susan. *Meeting and Event Planning for Dummies.* Hoboken, NJ: Wiley, 2003.

Mancuso, Jennifer. *The Everything Guide to Being an Event Planner: Insider Advice on Turning Your Creative Energies into a Rewarding Career.* Avon, MA: Adams Media, 2008.

Market Research Media, Inc. "Virtual Conference & Trade Show Market Forecast 2013–2018." Retrieved January 20, 2014 (http://www.marketresearchmedia.com/?p=421).

Moran, Jill S. *How to Start a Home-based Event Planning Business.* Third ed. Guilford, CT: Globe Pequot Press, 2010.

Salary.com. "Most Popular Cities for Meeting/Event Planner." Retrieved January 17, 2014 (http://swz.salary.com/SalaryWizard/event-planner-Salary-Details.aspx).

Savas, Lisa Plummer. "The Rookie Diaries." Retrieved January 8, 2014 (http://connectyourmeetings.com/2013/11/19/the-rookie-diaries).

Schwartz, Ellen. Interview with the author. January 5, 2014.

Silvers, Julia Rutherford. *Professional Event Coordination.* New York, NY: Wiley, 2012.

Sloan, Sandy. Interview with the author. January 2, 2014.

Successful Meetings. "The Top 10 Cities for Planner Jobs." Retrieved January 17, 2014 (http://www.successfulmeetings.com/Event-Planning/SM-Top-10/Articles/The-Top-10-Cities-for-Planner-Jobs).

Suckow, Shawna. *Planner Pet Peeves: Straight Talk for Meetings Industry Suppliers to Understand How Planners Really Think, Act and Buy.* Self-published, 2012.

Ting, Deanna. "7 More Predictions About the Future of Meetings." Successful Meetings. Retrieved January 9, 2014 (http://www.successfulmeetings.com/print.aspx?id=17266).

Wolf, Paulette, Jodi Wolf, and Donielle Levine. *Event Planning Made Easy.* New York, NY: McGraw-Hill, 2005.

index

ABOUT THE AUTHOR

Barbara Krasner holds a master's degree in marketing from the Rutgers School of Business in New Jersey. She has more than thirty years of experience in managing and staffing trade shows, corporate meetings, conferences, and workshops. A former marketing director in the telecommunications industry, she now focuses on planning and hosting events for writers world-wide. She makes sure she wears comfortable clothing on the day of any event because attendees always need something, speakers may get caught in traffic, and the microphone may not work.

PHOTO CREDITS